PARK LIFE

MICK CLEWES

Park Life: copyright © Mick Clewes 2024

All rights reserved. The moral rights of the artist/author have been asserted.

www.1889books.co.uk

ISBN: 978-1-915045-40-9

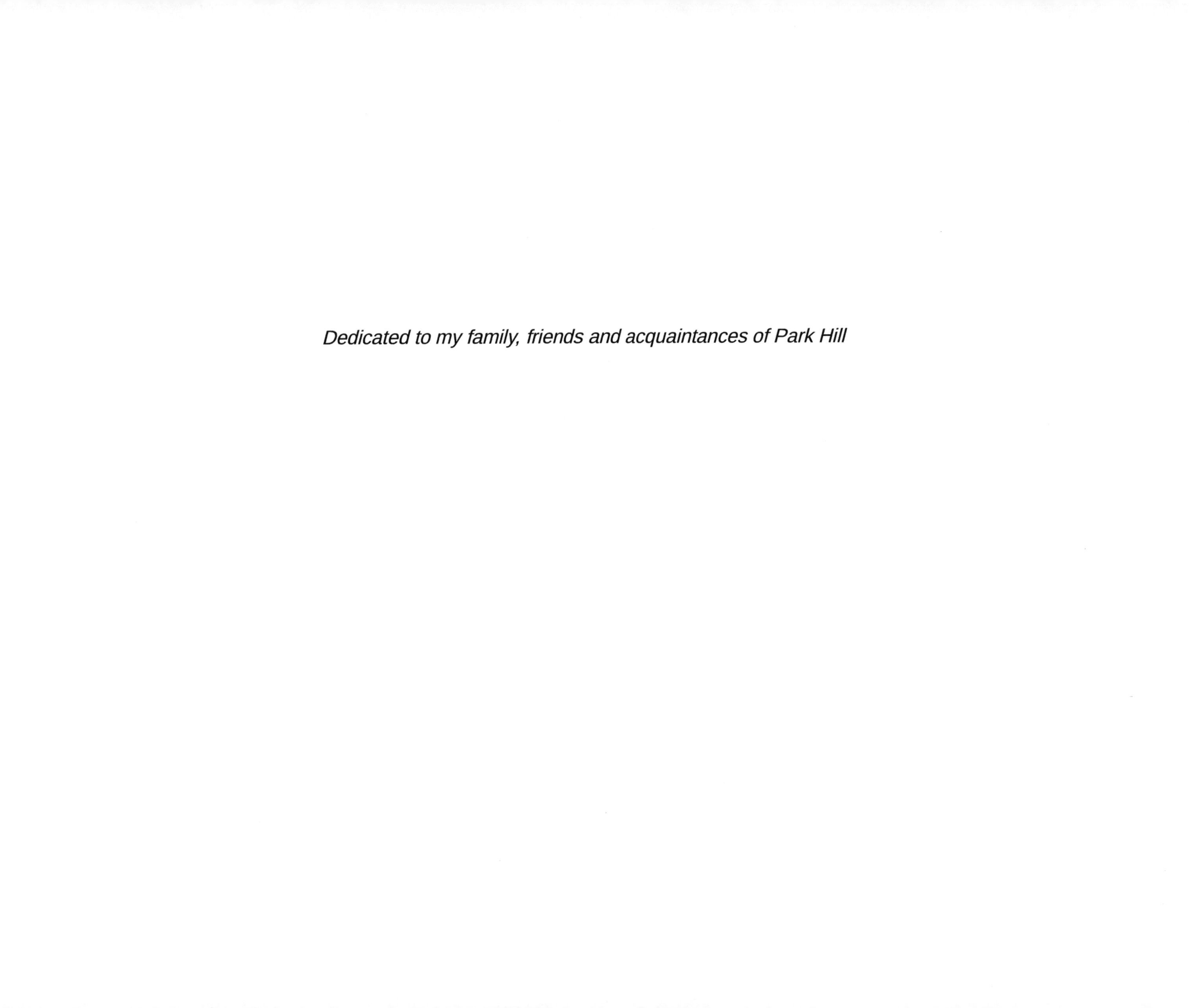

Dedicated to my family, friends and acquaintances of Park Hill

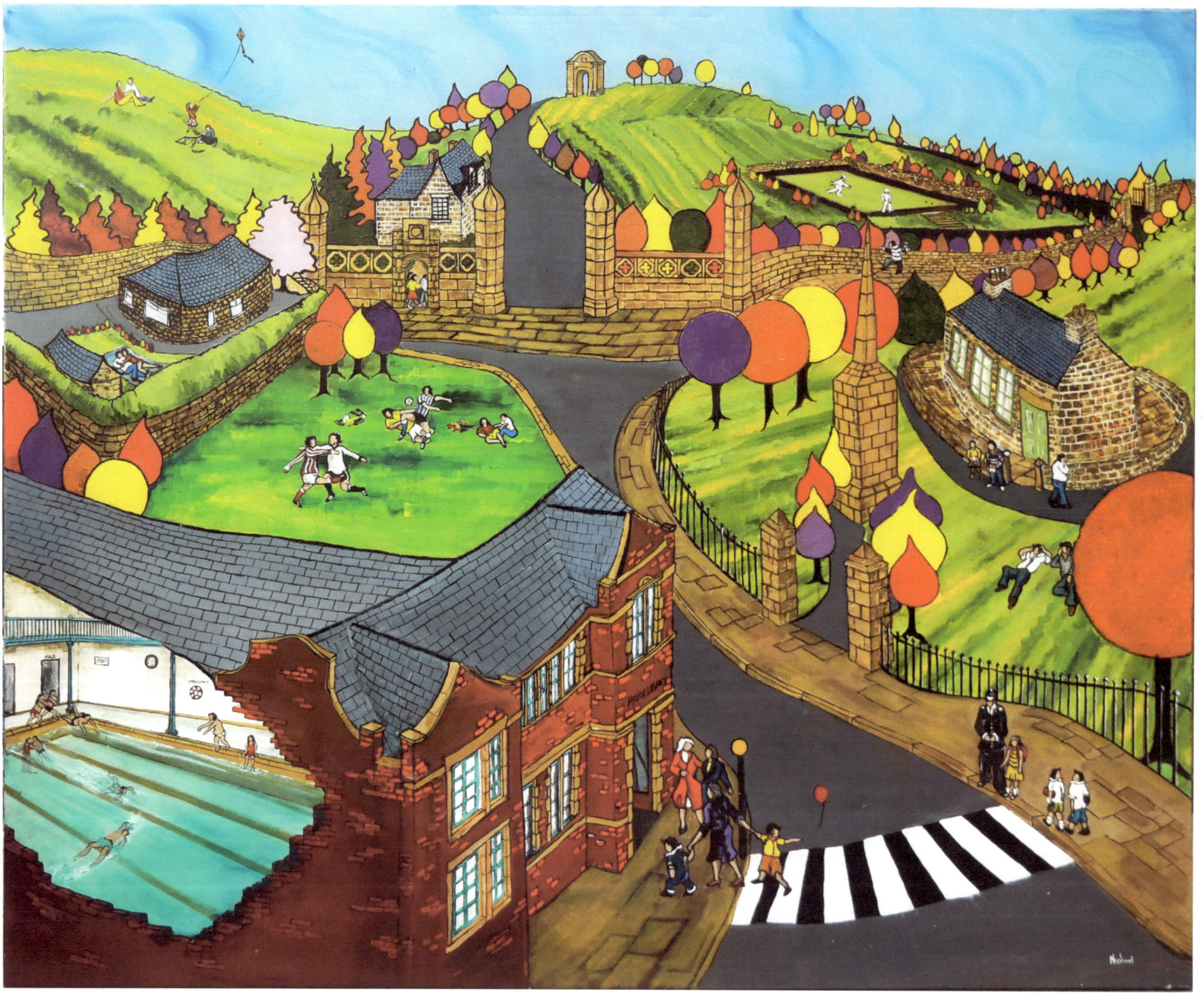

INTRODUCTION – JUST A LAD FROM PARK HILL

My family moved to Park Hill around 1961 when I was a year old.

It is difficult for some people who have not lived on Park Hill or have little knowledge of life there to understand the connection many have with the area. Yes, the building can be considered brutal, and grey, but the complex was a major improvement for many families that moved from the "slums." They and others who were welcomed in, created a community, long lasting friendships and acquaintances that last to this day. That is testament to the success of Parkhill.

We didn't see a brutal building, but, for us children: one massive playground, families looking out for each other. There were playgrounds, grassed areas, football yards, shopping centres, pubs, community centre, organised sport days, coach trips, Bingo, Friday night discos, and of course, indoor toilets!

After a working life in the construction industry, firstly as a joiner, eventually becoming a construction site manager, I decided to retire, with the intention of progressing my art. I then decided to try and capture some moments in time, of my life around the Park area. There is a little bit of me in some of my paintings, but hopefully others will see themselves too: not physically but hopefully in the memories that my paintings reawaken.

It seems to me that Sheffield, like Park Hill, gets a bad press sometimes: like some people of Sheffield having nothing good to say of Park Hill, so too some people from other areas of the country when it comes to the city itself. Through my paintings I have attempted to show the buildings and the skies as perceived by others both of Park Hill and Sheffield: a little bleak, grim, rather dark. But, by painting the people in a more colourful way, I try to reflect their character: despite the toil and bad times, the people are resilient, vibrant and know how to enjoy themselves.

I have always drawn, or tried to make things, from an early age. I am basically self-taught, just the odd evening class, no set technique, it either turns out or it doesn't!

Here begins a little journey of the Park area (and beyond) through my paintings set around the 60's and 70's, alongside little anecdotes some amusing hopefully, some rekindling memories of the Park district, the people and in particular the residents of Park Hill flats.

– MC 2024

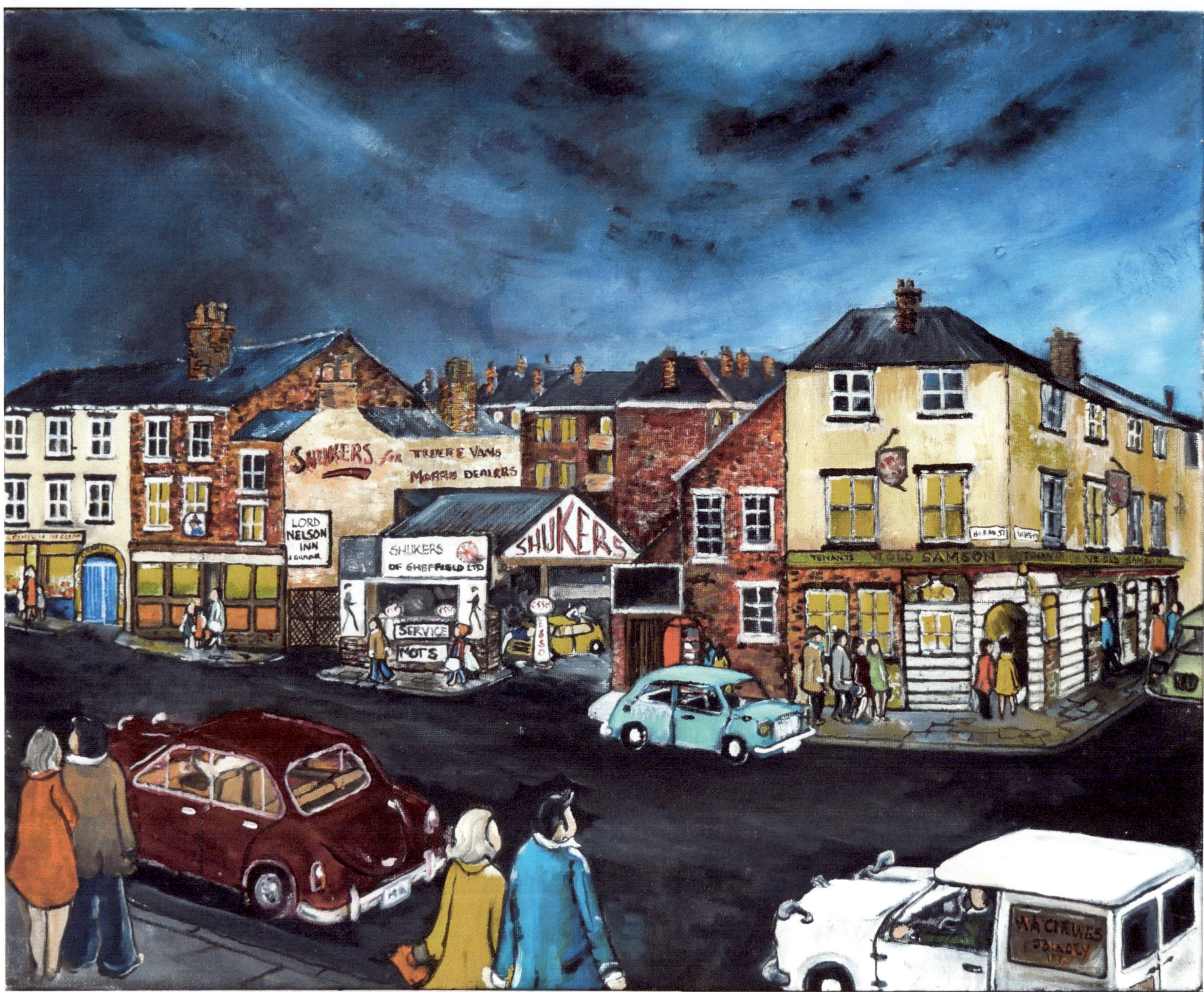

SHUKERS for TRUCKS & VANS
MORRIS DEALERS
SHUKERS
LORD NELSON INN
SHUKERS OF SHEFFIELD LTD
SERVICE
MOTS
TENANTS OLD SAMSON
HEAD ST

Broad Street and Granelli's

Broad St was once a busy road which led more or less up past the market, and up to Dixon Lane. were the Park Square roundabout sits today.

It had numerous Pubs: Ye old Samson, The Nelson, Ye old Harrow, and The Durham Ox. Its shops were what we'd call independent now. Violet Mays, record shop was probably the most well known.

My dad would sometimes take us down to the Old Harrow, and sit us outside with a packet of crisps with a little blue package containing salt flavour and a bottle of pop. If we had any pocket money we would pop down to Granellis for some sweets, or an ice cream, then round to the playground on Crown Alley. It had the biggest slide you ever saw, rocking horse, merry go round and see saw. There was hop scotch tiggy, and skipping too.

Dad would continue the pub crawl of course.

"We would go down sometimes with a bowl to get some ice cream from Granellis and take it back home, if it wasn't a bowl it might have been pram, to fill it with coal from Shukers."

Granelli's

Granelli's sweet shop was a Park institution and is still going to this day

"There were so many sweets to choose from: bourbons, midget gems, sherbert dip and more. My favourites were coconut mushrooms. We would walk back up to the flats; I remember the smell of freshly baked bread from Arbors bakery."

"You could take a bowl in and get it filled with ice cream to take home, happy days"

"Every kind of sweet you could think of, would get 2oz and then go round to playground at the back."

"At their stall in the market you could get a big bag of broken biscuits for next to nowt"

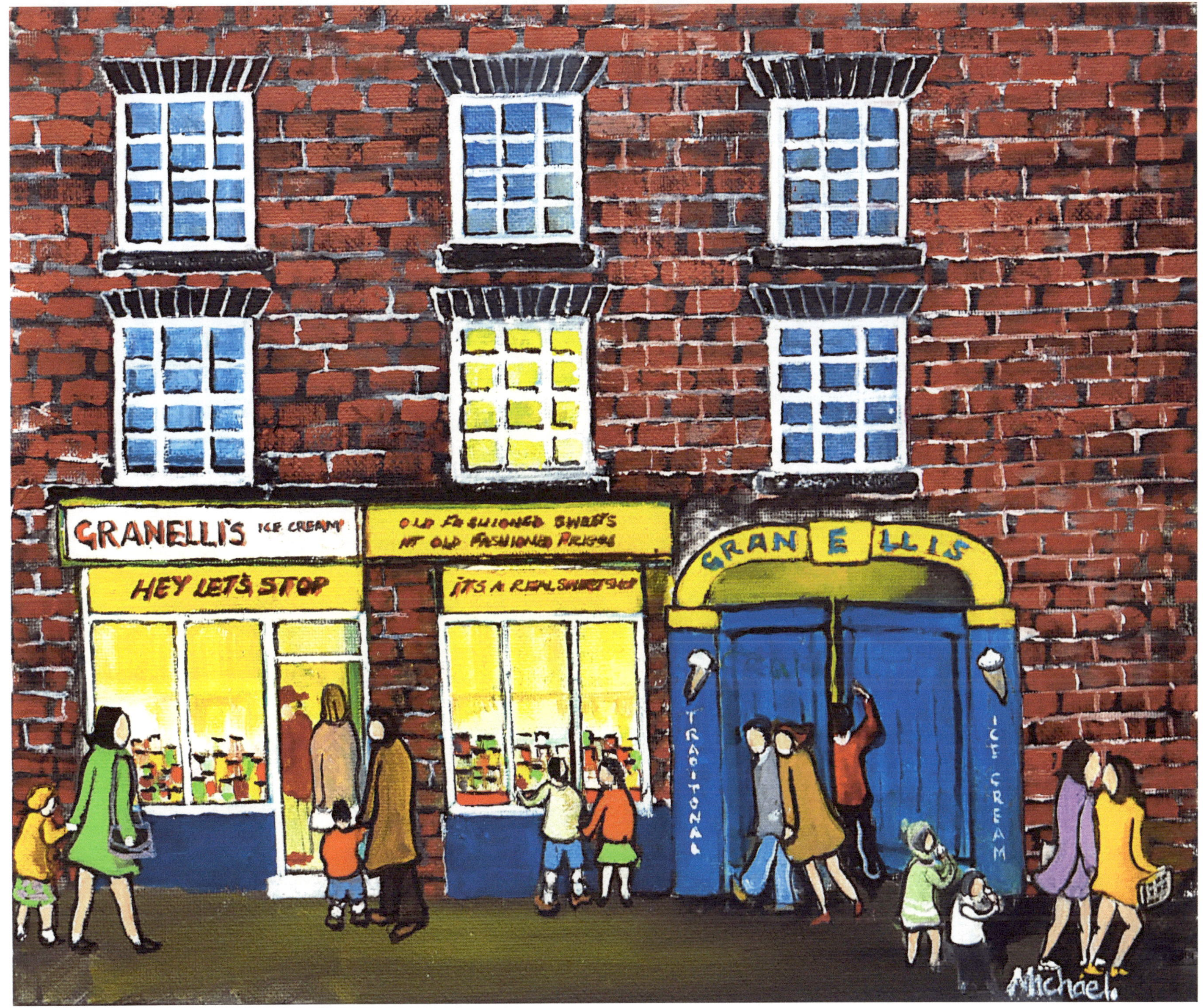

GRANELLI'S ICE CREAM
OLD FASHIONED SWEETS AT OLD FASHIONED PRICES
HEY LETS STOP
ITS A REAL SWEETSHOP
GRAN E LLIS
TRADITIONAL
ICE CREAM
Michael.

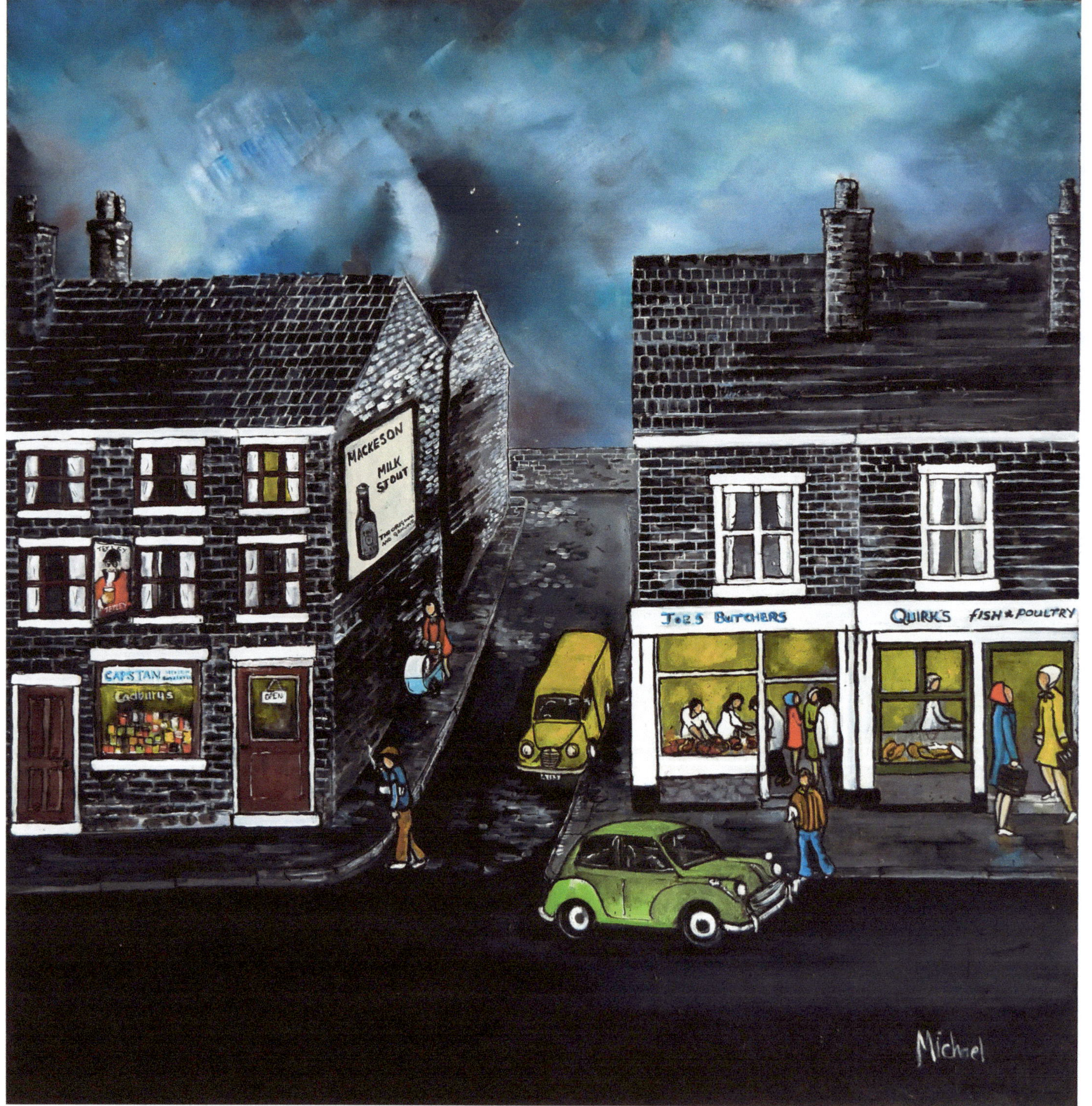

MACKESON
MILK STOUT
CAPSTAN
Cadbury's
OPEN
JOES BUTCHERS
QUIRK'S FISH & POULTRY
Michael

Duke Street Shops

When I got to around the age of 11 and could cross the road safely, I had the enviable task of fetching the bones from Joe's butchers, to make the Sunday gravy, it seemed like some form right of passage passed down the family,brother to brother. Oh the shame of it all! It did make good gravy mind you, and I could strip the meat of the bone after!

I remember arranging to go out with this girl from school. We both knew, the girl who lived in the beer off opposite the flats. I borrowed my older brother's star jumper, hoping to impress, and ran round the landing to check she was there. I got a thumbs up from both of them stood in the window. It was a go: happy summer 1975.

Talbot Street Shops

The Trades and Labour Club now stands on the area to the left.

There was Walkers off licence, Swallows sweets, Simmonites newsagents and more.

On Saturday evenings, paperboys would be hanging around waiting for Green 'un to arrive, bags at the ready, chewing a Bazooka Joe gum and reading the little story on the wrapper. Pay day when you got back: around 19 bob if you had delivered mornings and evenings. You'd buy a comic: Beano, Dandy , Hotspur, then over to Swallows for a bag of sweets: gob stoppers, barley twist, peanut brittle or a Jubilee ice lolly, all set to share. Then home and back out for mum and dad's last minute needs before a night out: lacquer for mum, razor blades for dad, Mackesons for Gran the baby sitter. Then later on a chicken supper.

Kids would go to Alf Walkers with a written note or two: "Please Alf can you serve my lad with twenty Embassy, or can you put it on tick and I will pay at the end of the week."

We would return pop bottles for around a penny a go, not a bad return to say we had probably pinched one or two off pop delivery man earlier in day.

You could put a shilling or two away in the firework club. Come bonfire night, we'd build a fire on any spare piece of land we could find, often getting wood from old furniture left out, or stripping out shelves, cupboards, from derelict houses and shops.

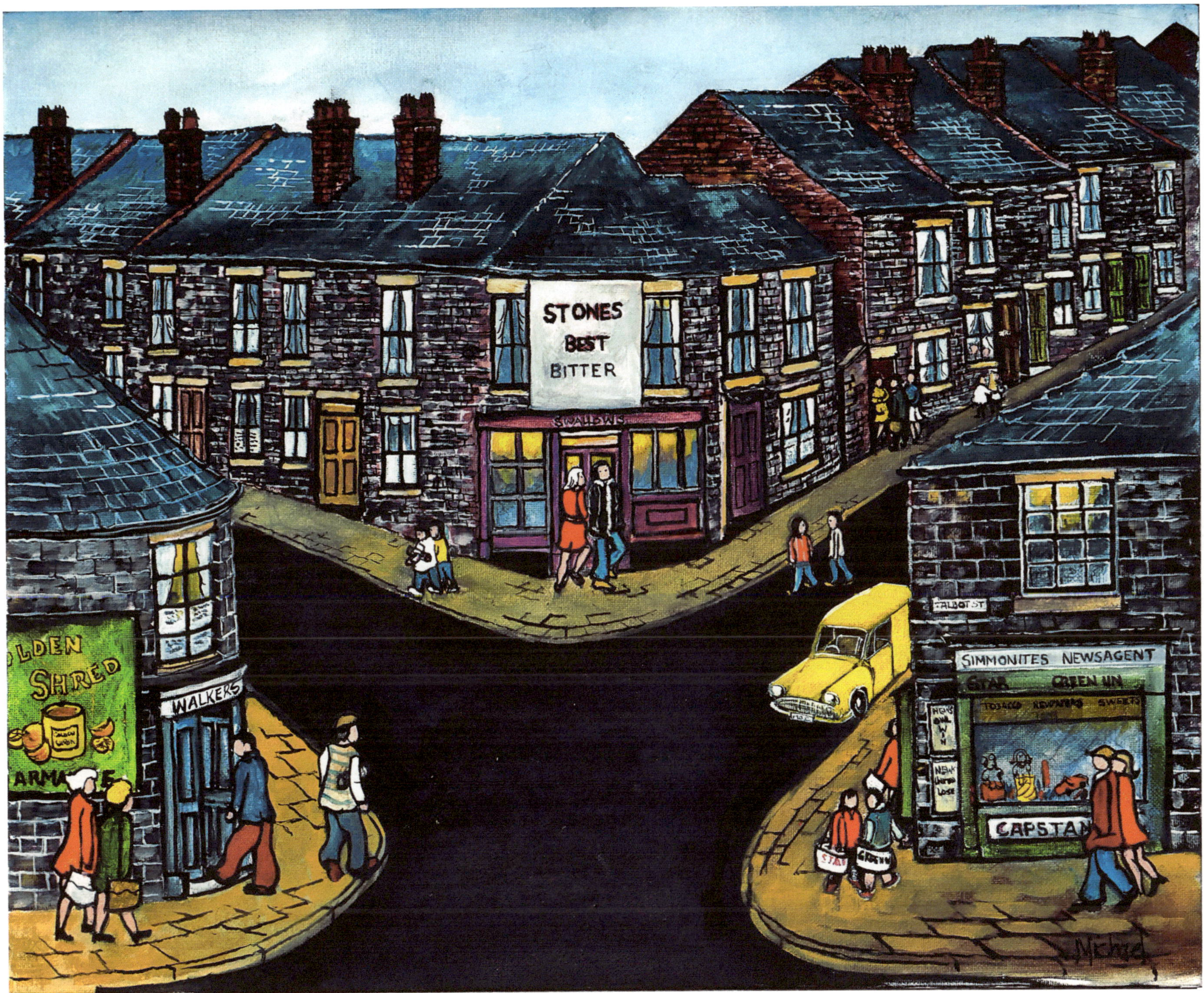
STONES
BEST
BITTER
SWALLOWS
GOLDEN
SHRED
MARMALADE
WALKERS
TALBOT ST
SIMMONITES NEWSAGENT
STAR   GREEN UN
TOBACCO NEWSPAPERS SWEETS
CAPSTAN

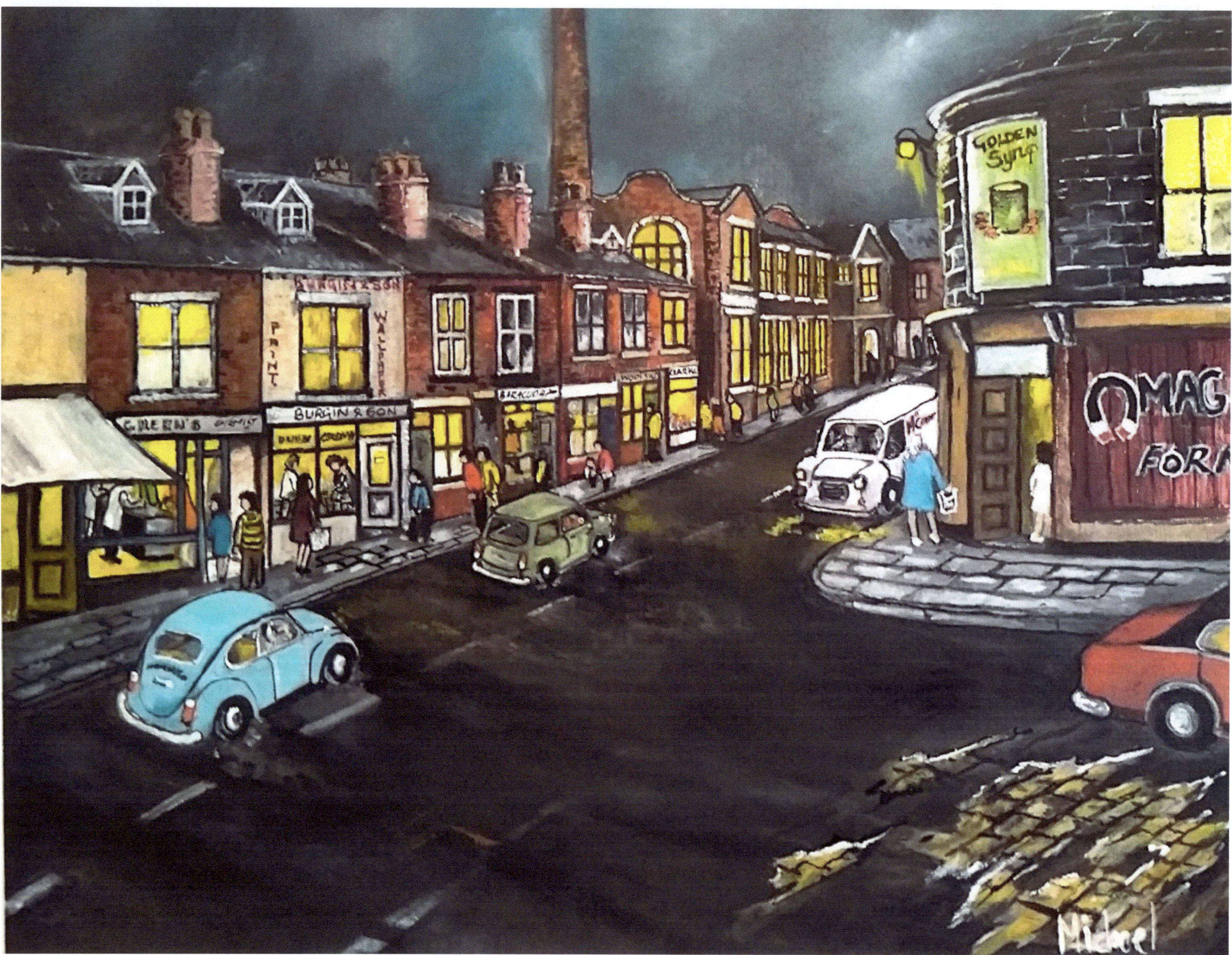

GOLDEN Syrup
GREEN'S CHEMIST
BURGIN & SON
PAINT
WALLPAPER
BURGIN & SON
BARACUDA
MAG
FOR
Michael

Park Baths

Duke Street had the Doctors, a Chemists, a Chinese takeaway, a decorators, the Barracuda fish bar, a Newsagaents and Off licence, and a pie shop.

A visit to the doctors was an experience: straight in, up to reception, give your name, take a seat if there was one, smoke seemed to fill the room. When you got into see the doctor, he would puffing away on his cigarette.

Many people will remember going to Park baths or the library. My mum would try and take us at least once a week to get new books from the library.

I remember once, my dad took us swimming, he dived in at the shallow end and as he did, his feet knocked off the warning board above.

My grandkids asked me once if we had showers then. "No, only a tin bath, or the slipper baths on Duke St. The baths had a big plug hole, if you weren't careful you would lose your flannel down it. The only showers we had were the rain type," I said.

"After going to Park baths, you could call in at the pie shop, well more of a front room than shop: knock on the door, walk in and get hot pork pie and peas, or Bovril, 2d a go, for the walk home.."

Park Pictures

"Empty PG tips packet would get you in half price, if you could afford PG tips that is, or you would get in through back door, sneak around on all fours until you got to the seats. Flash Gordon on Saturday morning!"

"When it turned to bingo hall, we won the jackpot one night, and bought our first car with winnings."

"When Mudfords closed we would go in, scrapping for lead – then off to weigh in, then maybe go down chippie to spend it."

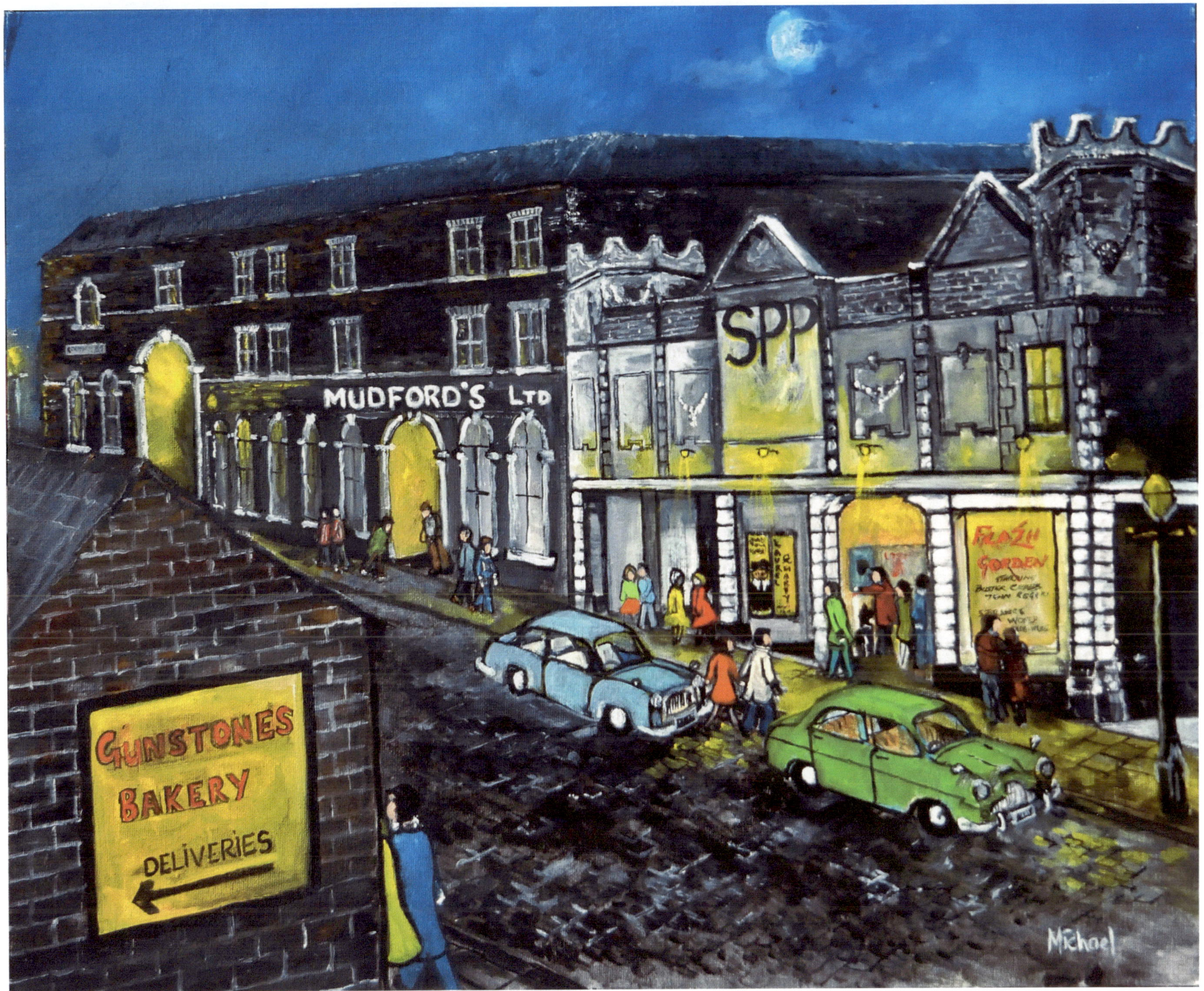

MUDFORD'S LTD
SPP
GUNSTONES
BAKERY
DELIVERIES
FLASH GORDEN
Michael

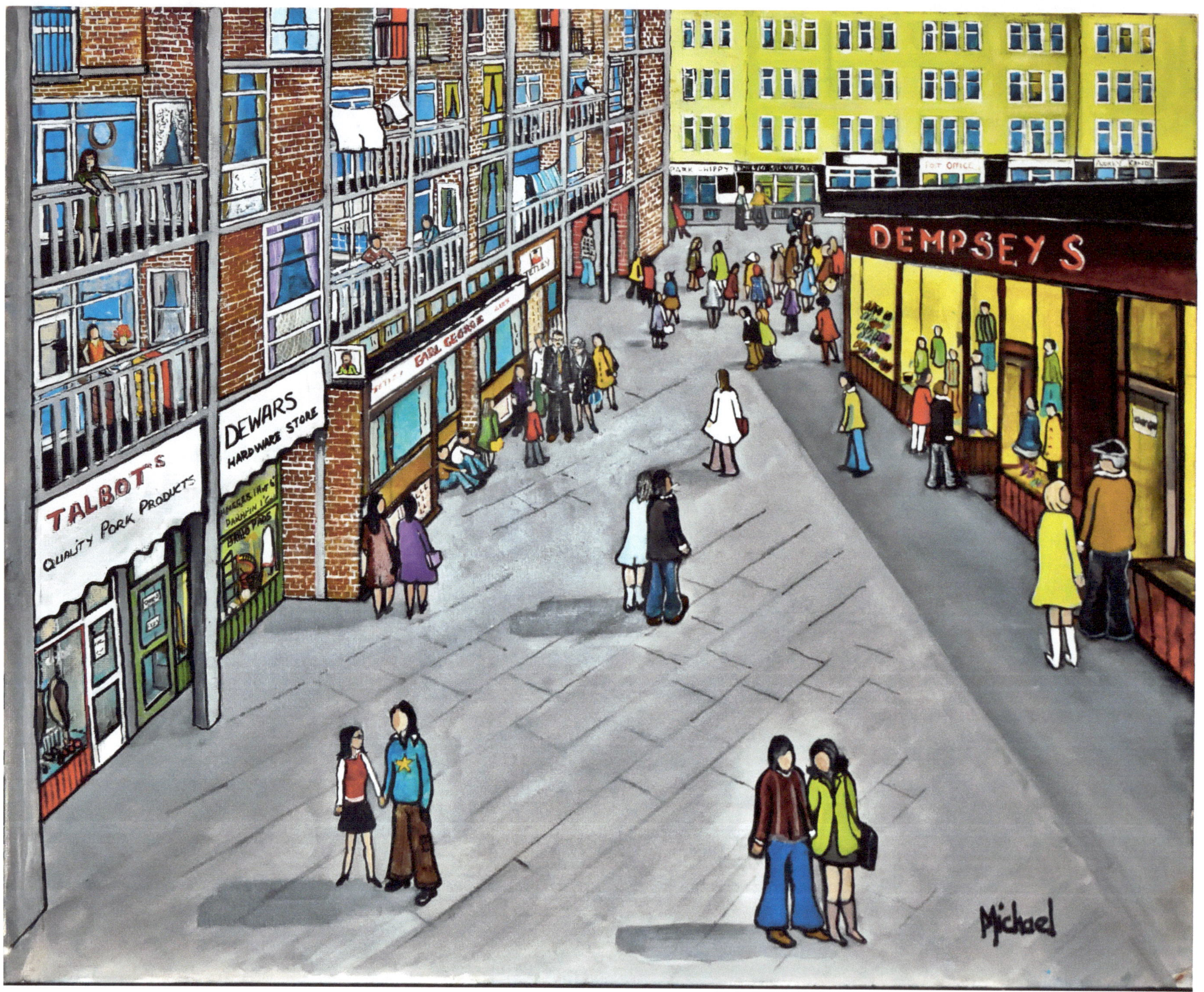
TALBOT's
QUALITY PORK PRODUKTS
DEWARS
HARDWARE STORE
EARL GEORGE
DEMPSEY S
POST OFFICE
Michael

Dempsey's

We got our school clothes from Dempsey's, usually paid for with cheques (paid back weekly – well, depending on the list of priorities – but it did get paid eventually). They had winkle pickers, monkey boots, beetle crushers and top dog football boots.

Come Whitsun, it was new clothes time. We went round the flats on the Sunday tapping on doors: "Hello, do you like my new clothes" we asked, got some smart comments, some swearing but also a copper or two, even a tanner or a bob. Didn't tell me mum though, she would have given me a right clip round the ear.

The Pavement Shopping Centre

The precinct had just about every shop you would need: food stores, newsagents, dentist, opticians, Dougies Barbers, toy and clothes store. It was more importantly a meeting place for a good chinwag. Chippie, A tanner's worth of chips, served up in newspaper, served three hungry lads, easy.

At the community hall there were Friday discos, live bands and bingo twice a week.

I remember one Saturday afternoon, my dad came home from the pub, a little flush. He took us all down to Hunters cycle store. My sister came out with a new pram, my younger brother a three wheeler bike. But for me and our big 'un, it was a snake belt apiece. A bloody snake belt! I ask you! I was never really sure where money came from. Sometimes it was best not to ask.

"I remember looking through the Zodiac coffee bar at the knickerbocker glories. I said to myself, one day when I get some money, I'm going to buy one of them." - Joan

"Had to do a delivery drop once to the Pavement shops. I asked this old fella, were the Pavements was. He just looked at me smirked and said, "What's tha think tha's stood on you daft bugger," and walked off. I couldn't help but laugh."

"I remember my step dad sending me to Talbots butchers for a pork hock. I was sweet and innocent then, what he actually said was to ask for a poor cock, the butcher and the rest of the shop just creased up." - Lynn

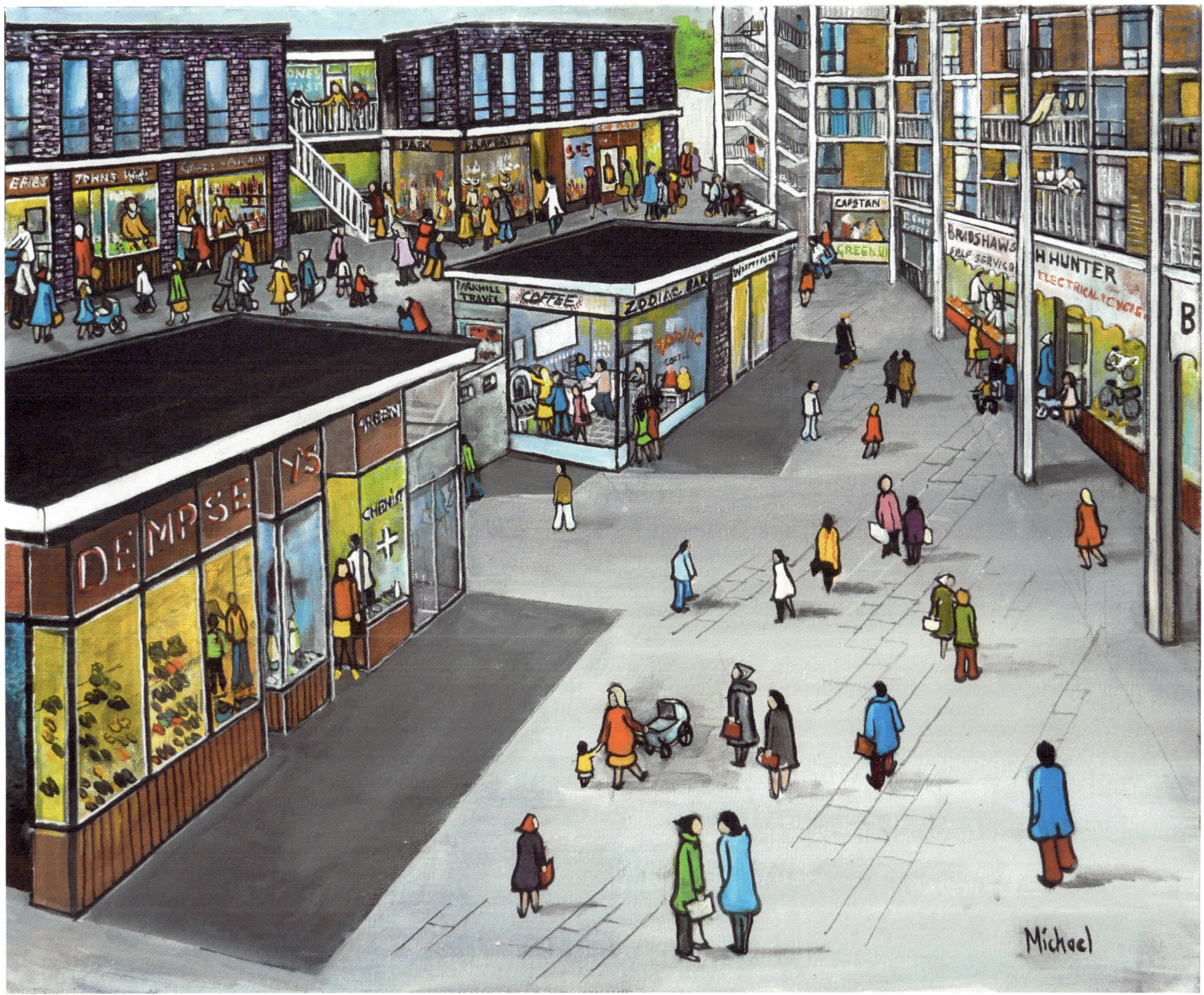

DEMPSEY'S
GREEN
CHEMIST
PARKHILL TRAVEL
KOFFEE
ZODIAC BAR
ZODIAC COFFEE
WHITTAKER
CAPSTAN
GREEN
BRADSHAWS
SELF SERVICE
H HUNTER
ELECTRICAL CYCLE
ERIBI
JOHN'S
JONES
Michael

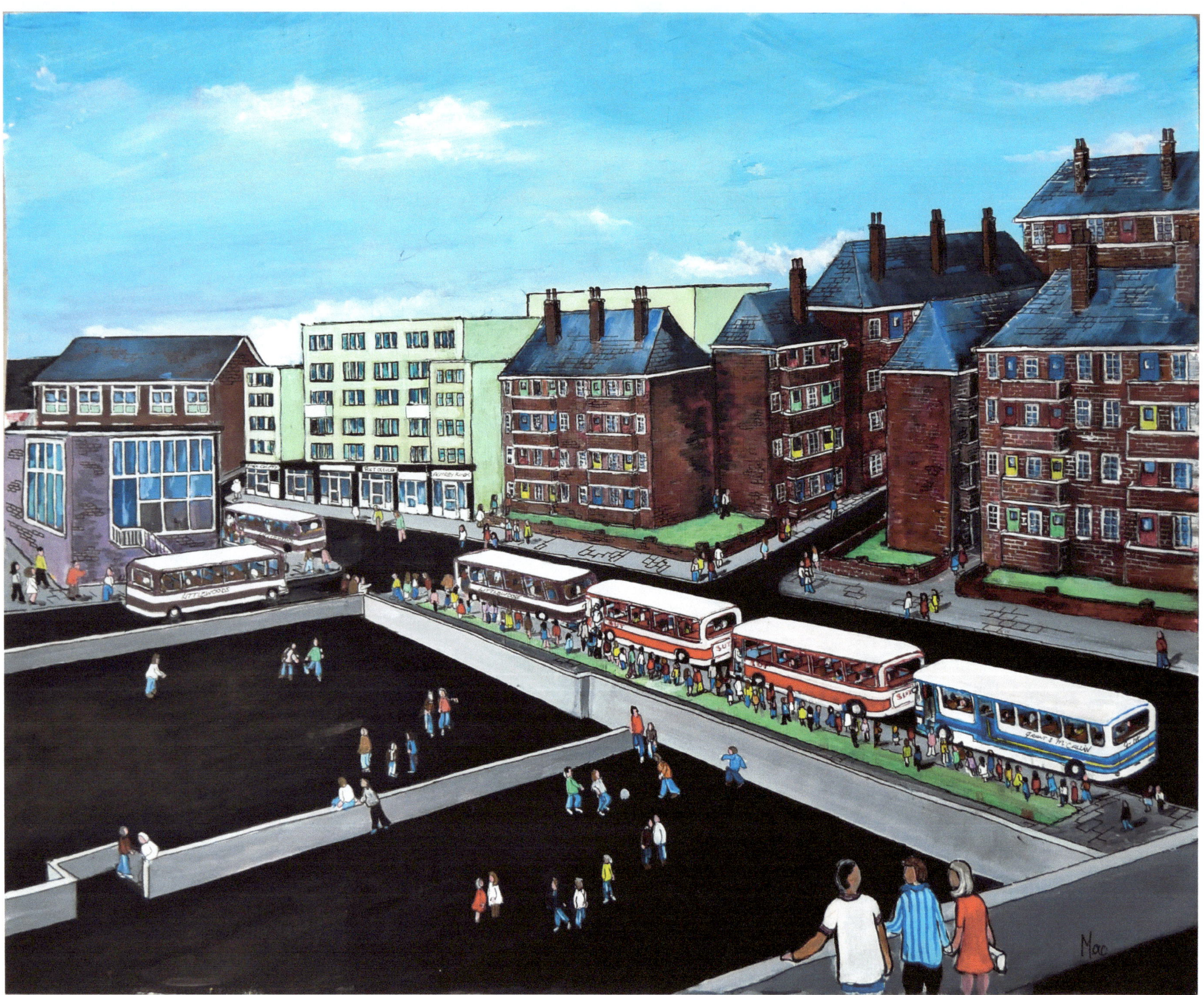

Day Trippers

Each summer, they organised a trip to Cleethorpes. Depending how many clubs your dad was a member of, you may have gone on quite a few.

"All the kids would be given a luggage label in case they got lost. There were separate coaches for adults. We'd get a packet of crisps, a bottle of pop, and ten bob to spend. No doubt the adults got a crate of beer for the trip."

"At tea time all the kids went to the Winter Gardens for tea – or was it a food fight!"

A Snowy Norfolk Park.

Although we had more than enough space on Park Hill to play, we also had Norfolk Park just up the road.

"Many a weekend in winter we would be up there, I remember once, me and my brother went down on the same sledge, just as we got to the bottom we did a belly flop, he landed on top of me. I'm sure I broke my nose!"

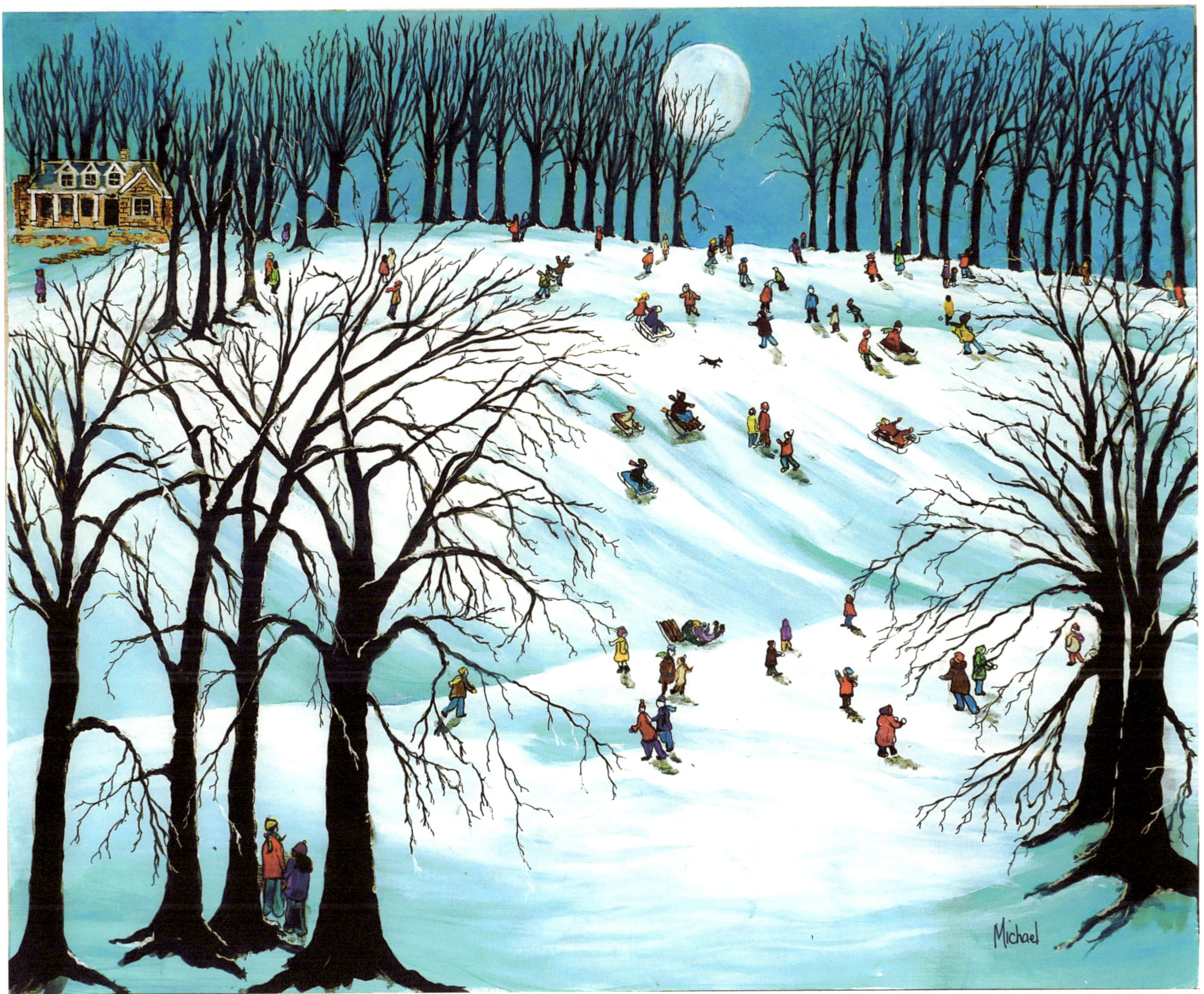
Michael

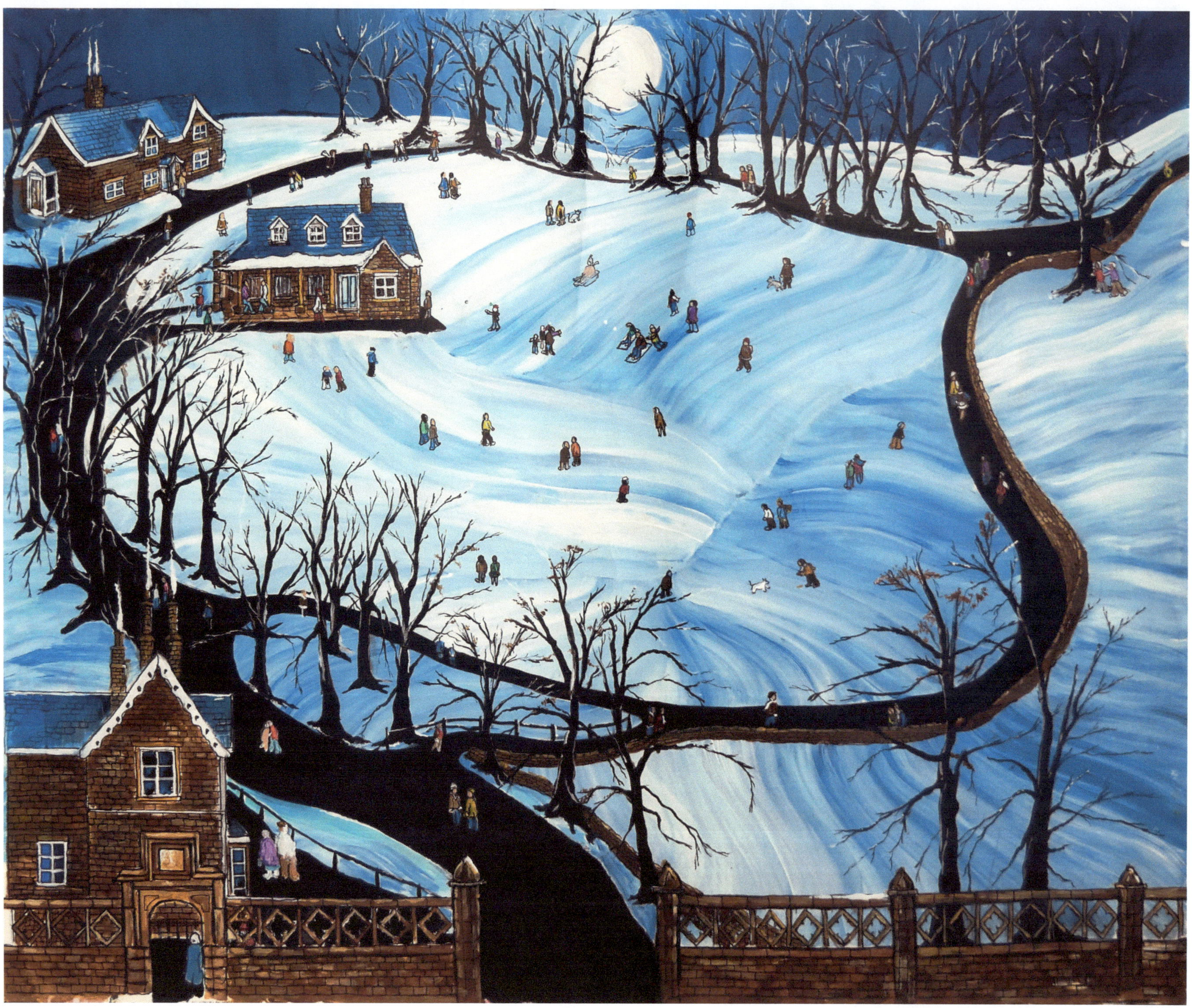

Snowy Norfolk Park II

Sledging at Bungay and the Old Sweet Factory

Bungay as we called it, around where the South Street amphitheatre is now.

Gloves if you were posh (!) or mittens threaded through your anorak, tied with elastic. If not you could improvise with a pair of old socks!

After we had been sledging we would call at the rock factory on Shrewsbury Road. More than once my Granddad would open the door. "What's tha want?" he asked. Always got a free bag of Yorkshire mixture, big fish, or rhubarb and custard, then off home!

"We would get an old car bonnet from the scrap yard just down the road, and sledge down to the bottom. Some even got hold of a car seat and strapped it to a bonnet. It went like a rat up a drain pipe." _Paul

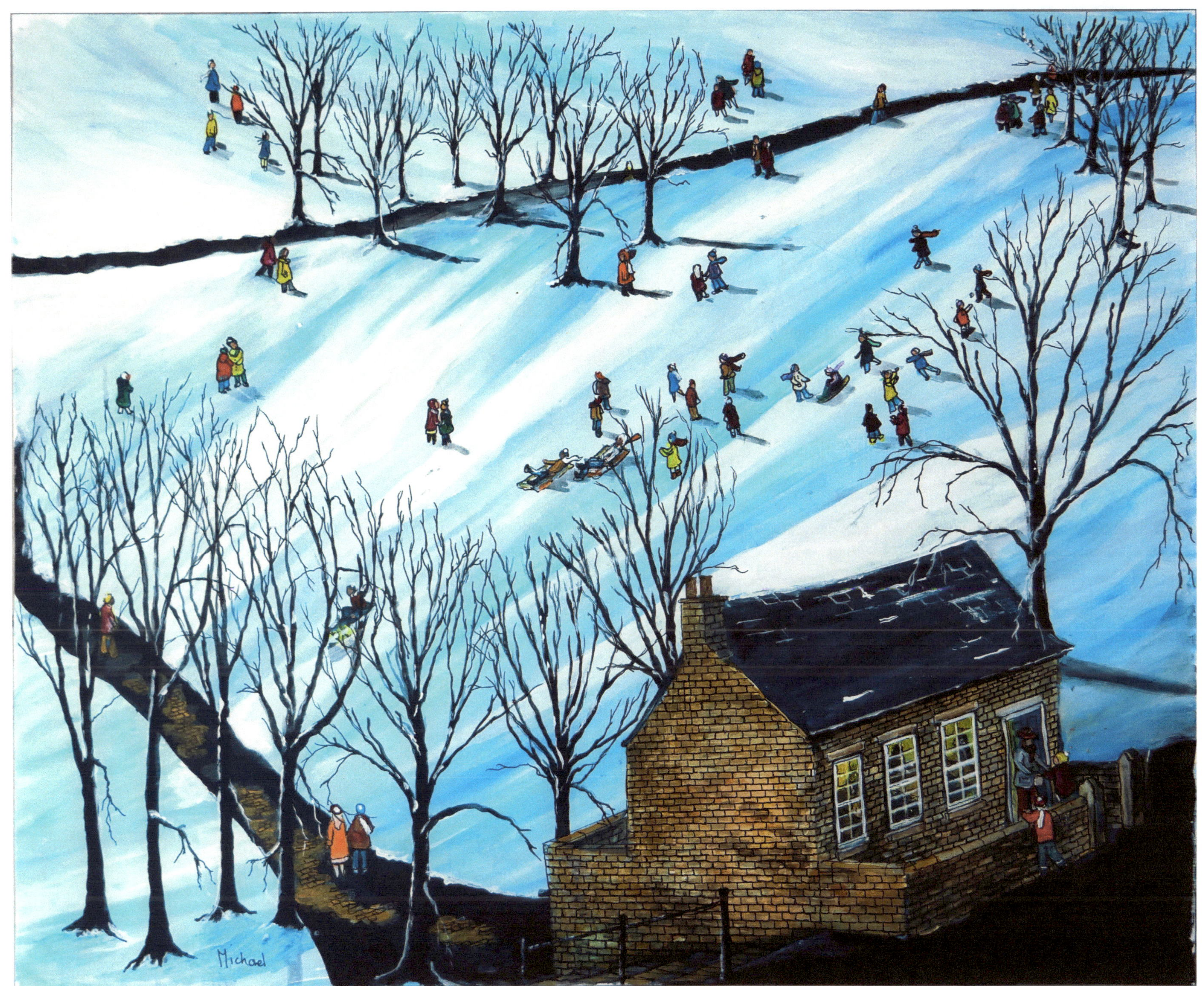

Michael

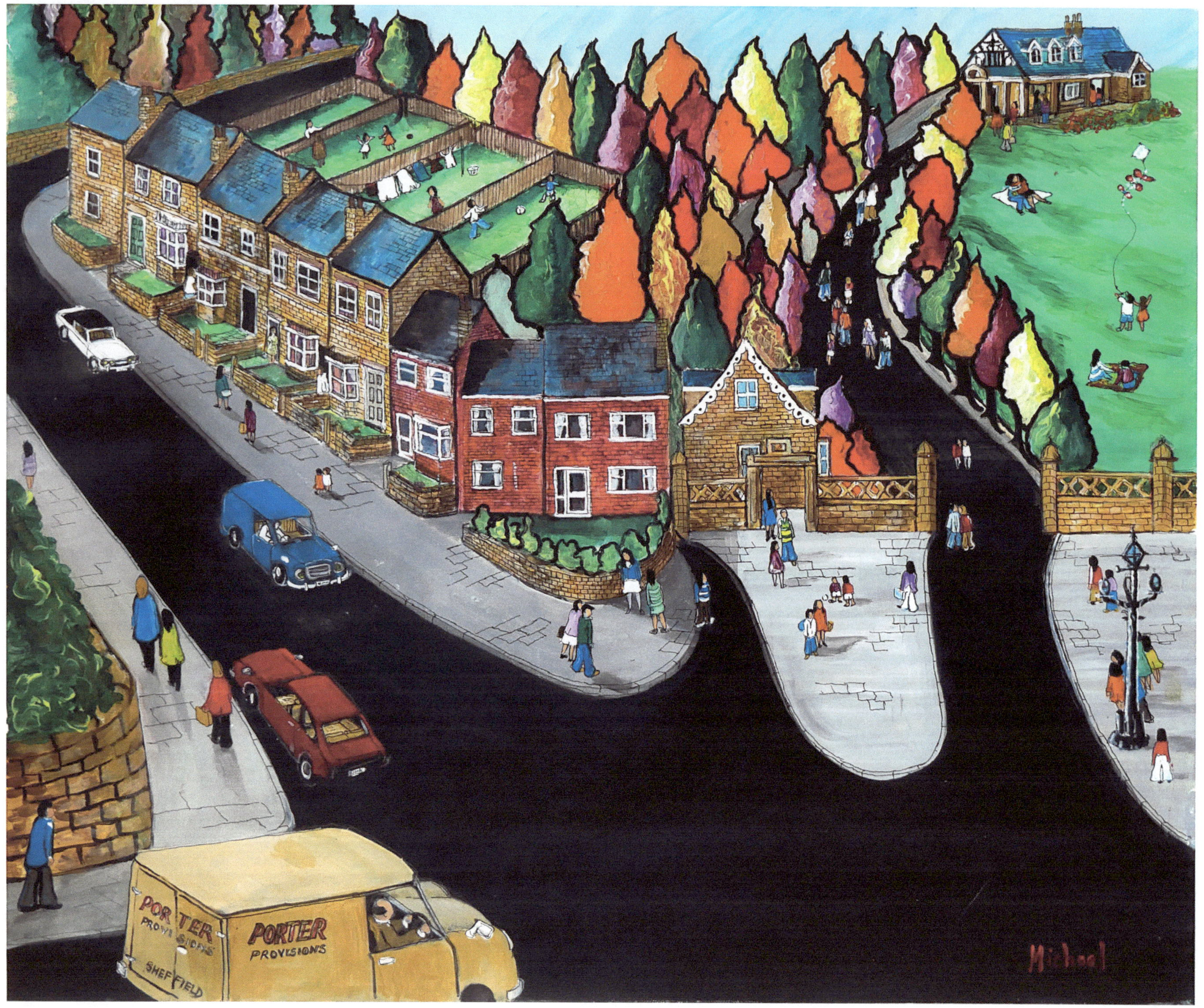
PORTER
PROVISIONS
SHEFFIELD
PORTER
PROVISIONS
Michael

Norfolk Park

Through out the year Norfolk Park, was a popular place.

We would walk through the park on our way home from school, tea and then meet up later on in the evening. Lazy evenings with friends, daisy chains, rolling down the hill, laughter, tennis, football, even a game of bowls occasionally, not sure how we found the time to revise for exams.

Norfolk Park and Norfolk Road

Whitsun parades, Bonfire nights, shows, fairs, and more
First kiss, first fag, carving names in trees, cafe for a Lyons maid ice cream: happy days!

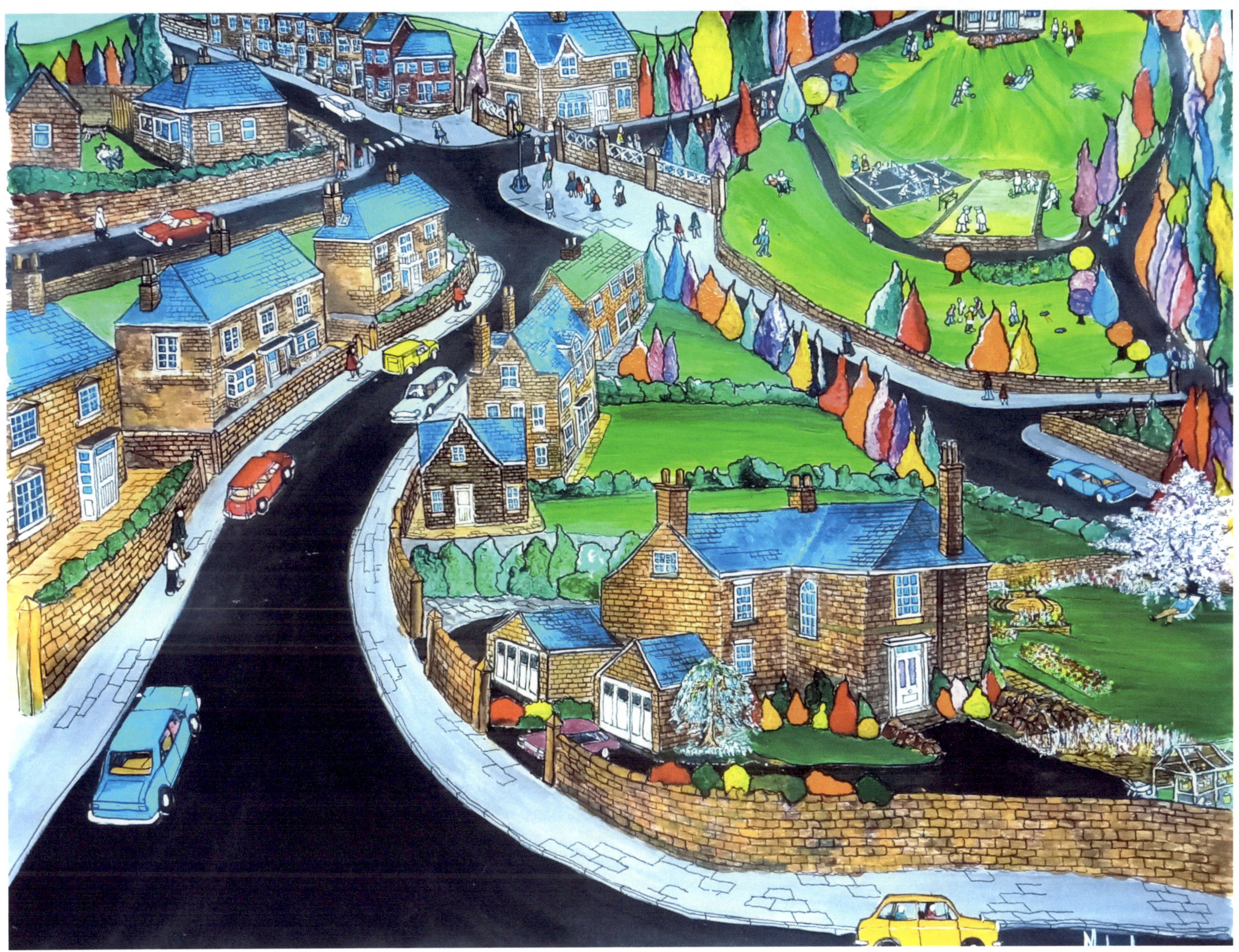

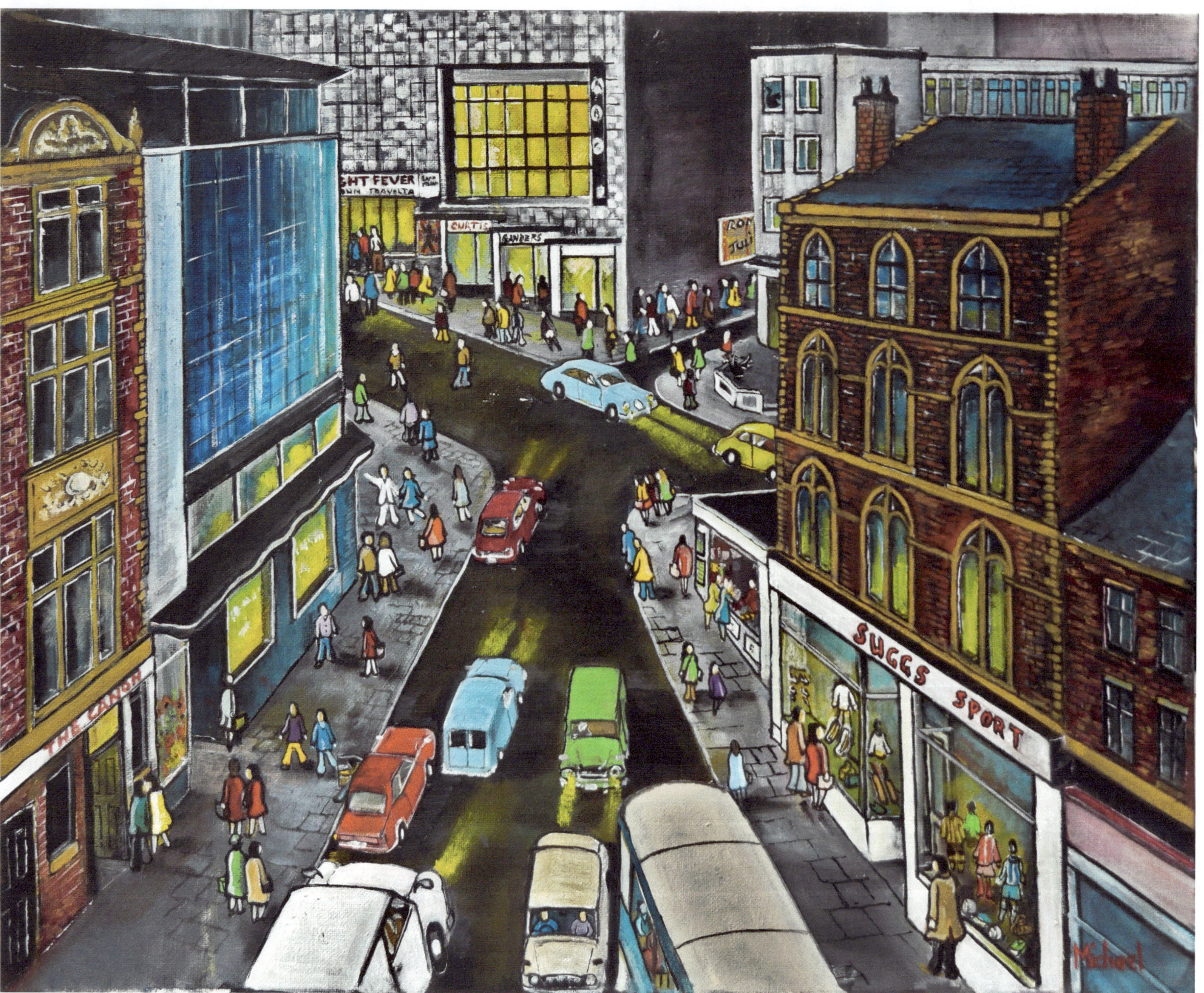
GHT FEVER
TRAVOLTA
CURTIS
GANDERS
ROM
JUL
THE CANON
SUGGS SPORT
Michael

The ABC Cinema, the Cannon, Co-op and Suggs

I took my girlfriend to see Saturday Night Fever, came out dancing, straight into Cannon Pub, where you went downstairs. Cowboy boots were the "in thing" at the time. After a drink or two, I got up to go. Walking across the floor, I thought to myself this floor feels uneven! I looked down and then round. My girlfriend was just stood there creased up laughing, as it seems was most of the pub: there was my missing heel in the middle of the floor, couldn't get out quick enough.

I swear the following Saturday, every fella in Top Rank, wore a medallion, with shirt undone down to the their belly button.

Sugg's sports was magic: it had everything you could need.

" I used to stand in Co-op doorway and look at the chicken roasting on the spit,: never got to sample one!"

The Classic, Fitzalan Square

I remember standing outside the Classic, waiting for a girl to turn up, all smart in my star jumper, with no coat. I waited ages, in the rain. She did turn up eventually, by then I looked like a drown rat. Not an impressive look. The Indus restaurant in Fitzalan Square was the place to go after a Saturday night session.

"My dad used to go down to Wigfalls every Saturday to pay the rental on the TV (well if he got past the pub and betting shop, that is."

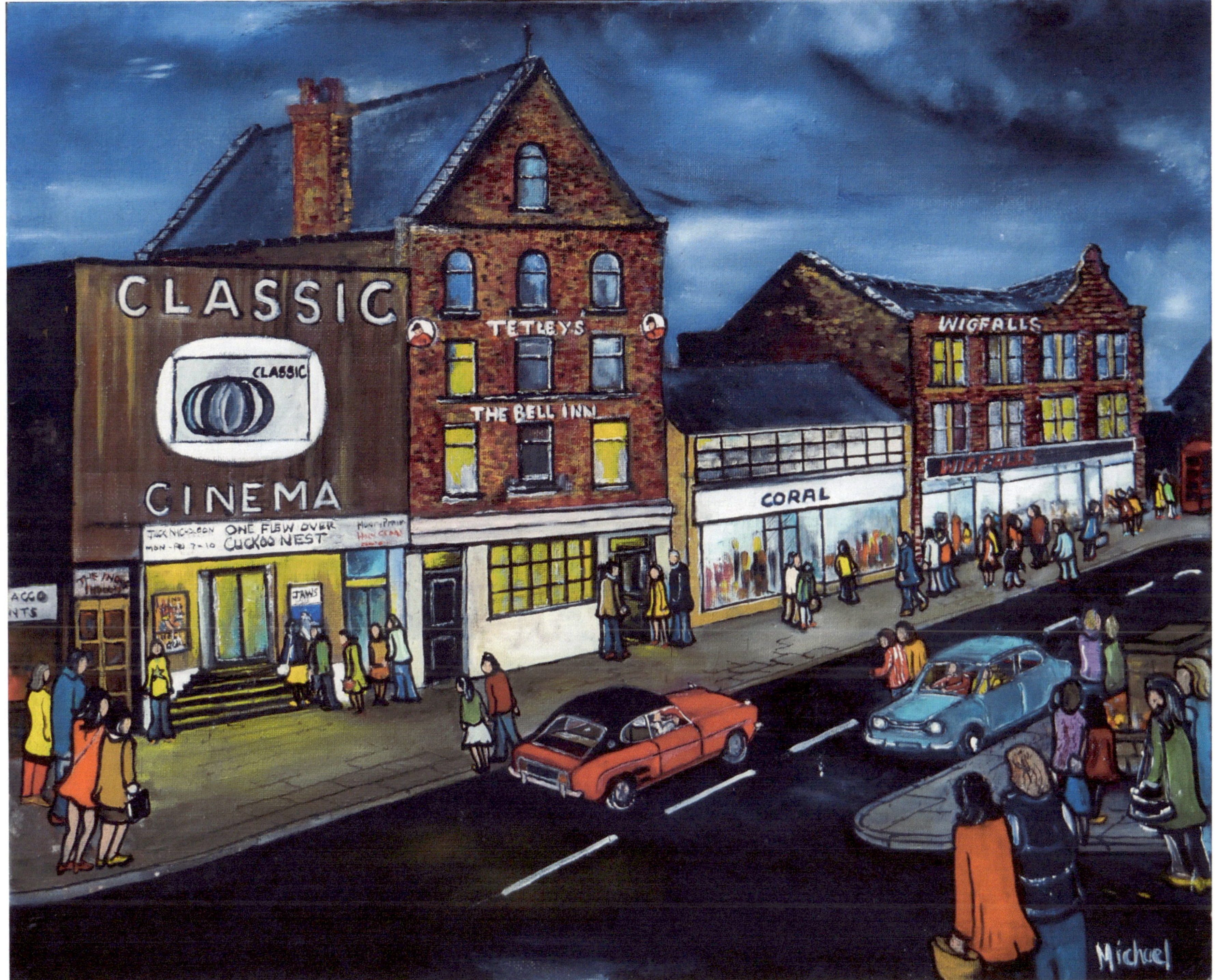

CLASSIC
CLASSIC
CINEMA
JACK NICHOLSON ONE FLEW OVER
MON-FRI 7-10 CUCKOO NEST
JAWS
TETLEY'S
THE BELL INN
CORAL
WIGFALLS
Michael

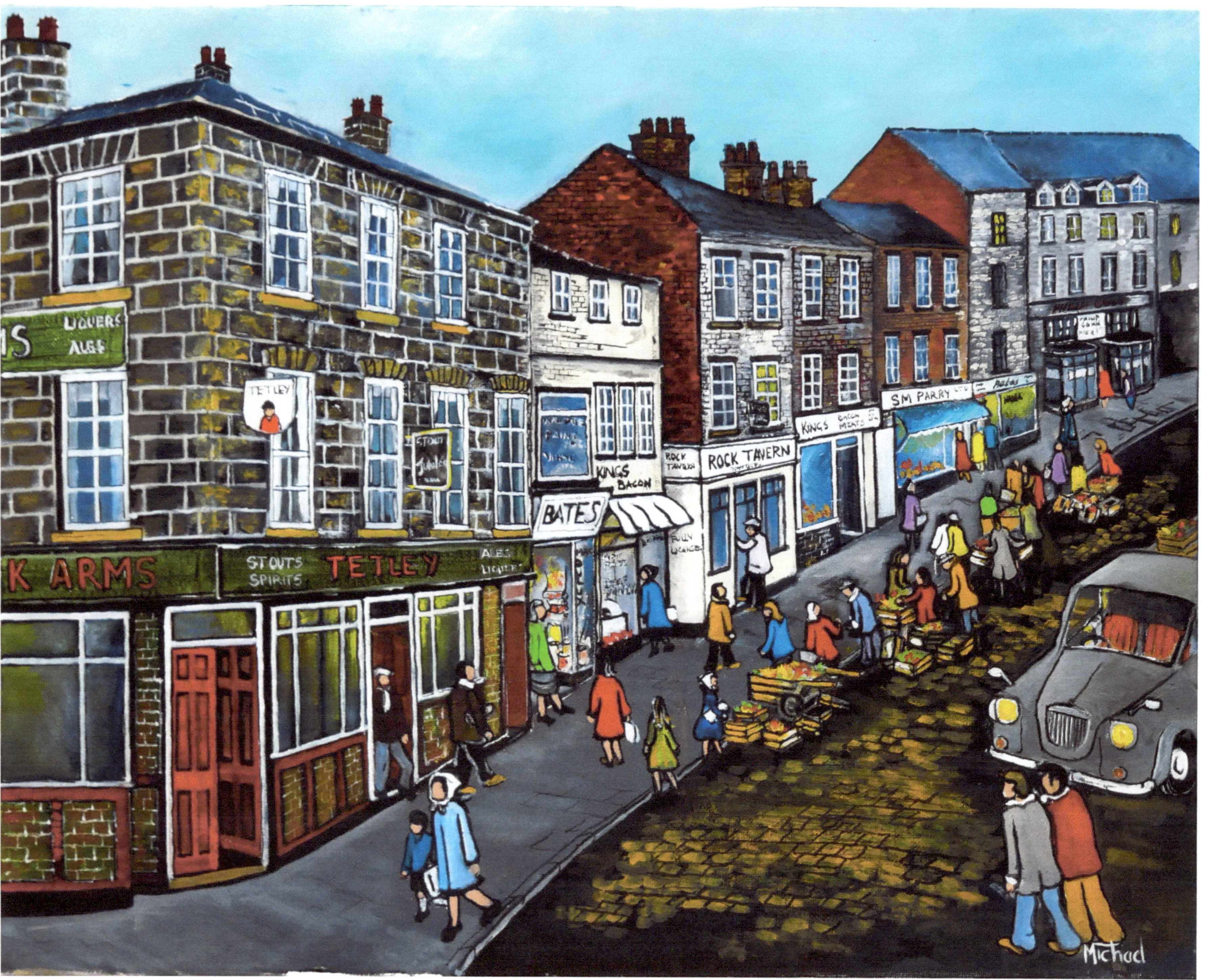
LIQUERS
ALES
TETLEY
STOUTS
Jubilee
K ARMS
STOUTS
SPIRITS
TETLEY
ALES
LIQUERS
BATES
KINGS
BACON
ROCK TAVERN
ROCK TAVERN
FULLY
LICENSED
KINGS
BACON
MEATS
SM PARRY
Michael

Dixon Lane

Home to Phillip Cann the Music Man, Kings where you could get the best pork sandwich, and stalls selling fresh fruit and veg. Me and our big un, would often head up into the markets and onto Dixon lane, always on the look-out for granddad to see if he had got a job on the stalls for the day. We knew we would get a freebie, if he had.

"Dad's local: me and mum would go shopping while dad went in pub. To be fair, he would come out and carry the shopping home."

Endcliffe Park

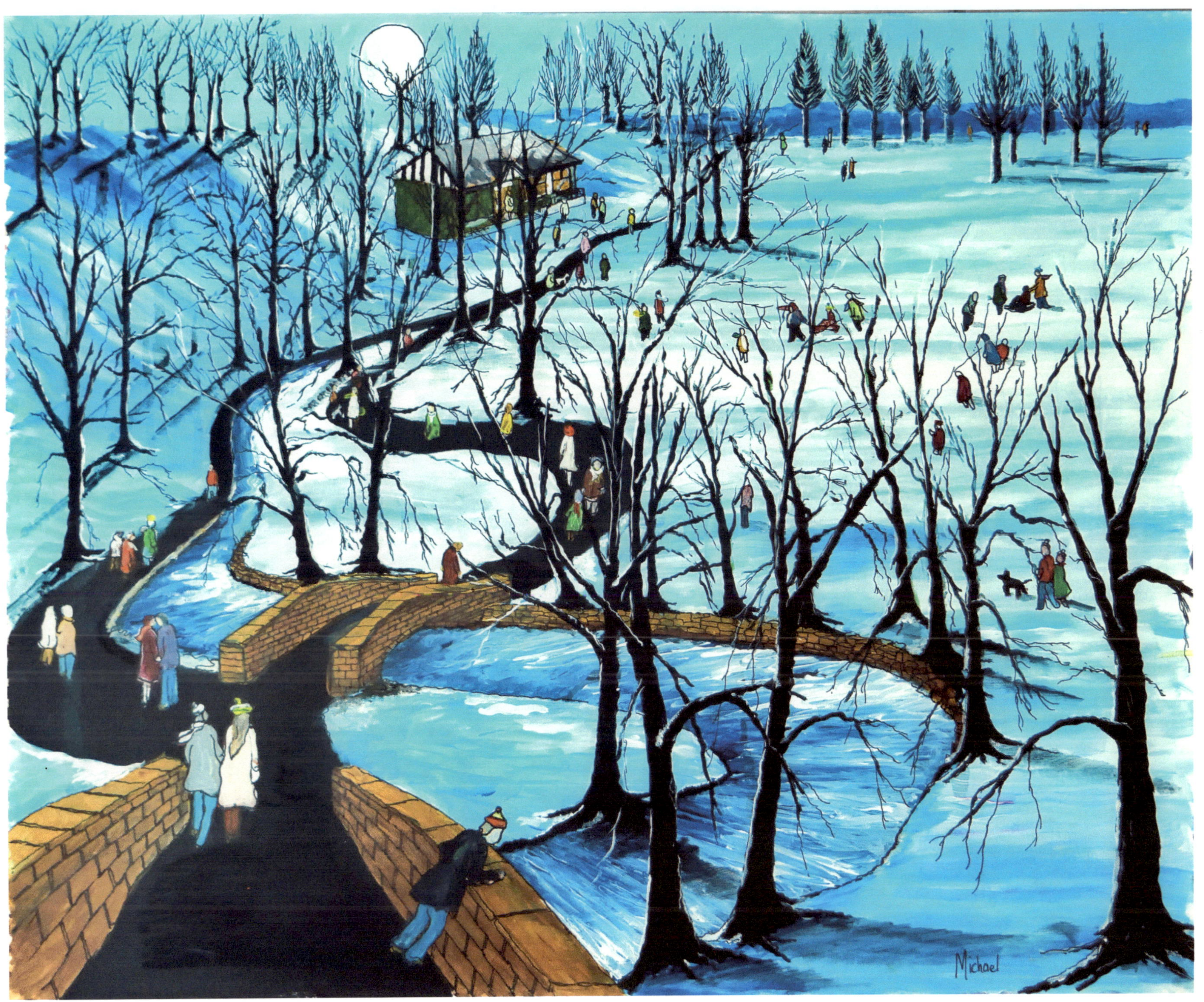
Michael

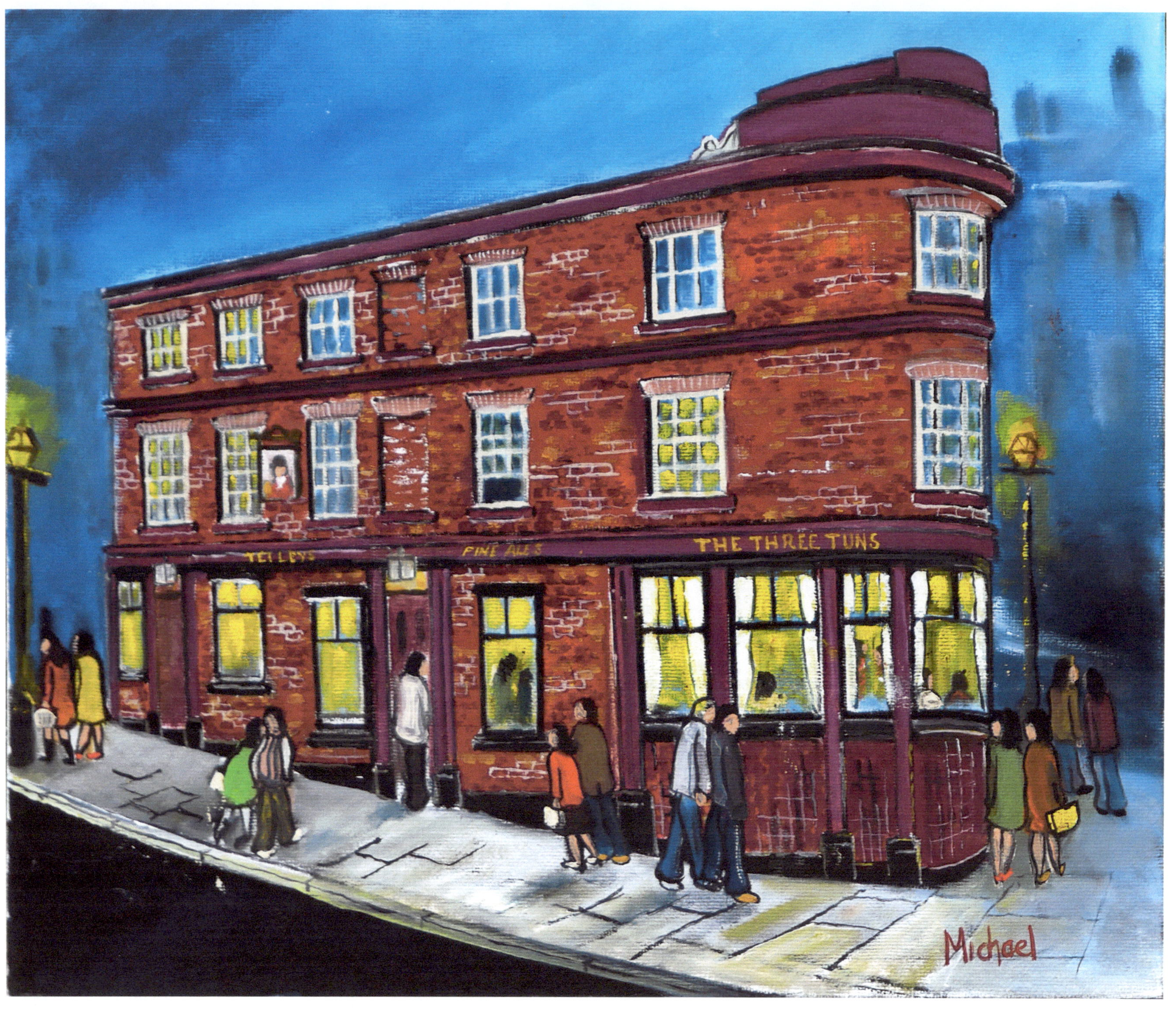

TETLEYS
FINE ALES
THE THREE TUNS
Michael

The Three Tuns

The Three Tuns, the Three Cranes, and the Blue Bell were regular Saturday routes, in the 70's early 80's. It was then off to a nightclub. Why I went to one I will never understand as I always ended up in a dark corner somewhere, much the worse for wear, until my mates picked me up when it was time to go home.

Henry's

From my time on Park Hill and my senior school days, friends have kept in touch, and we continue to meet up today. Henry's was a regular meeting place until the recent revamp of the area.

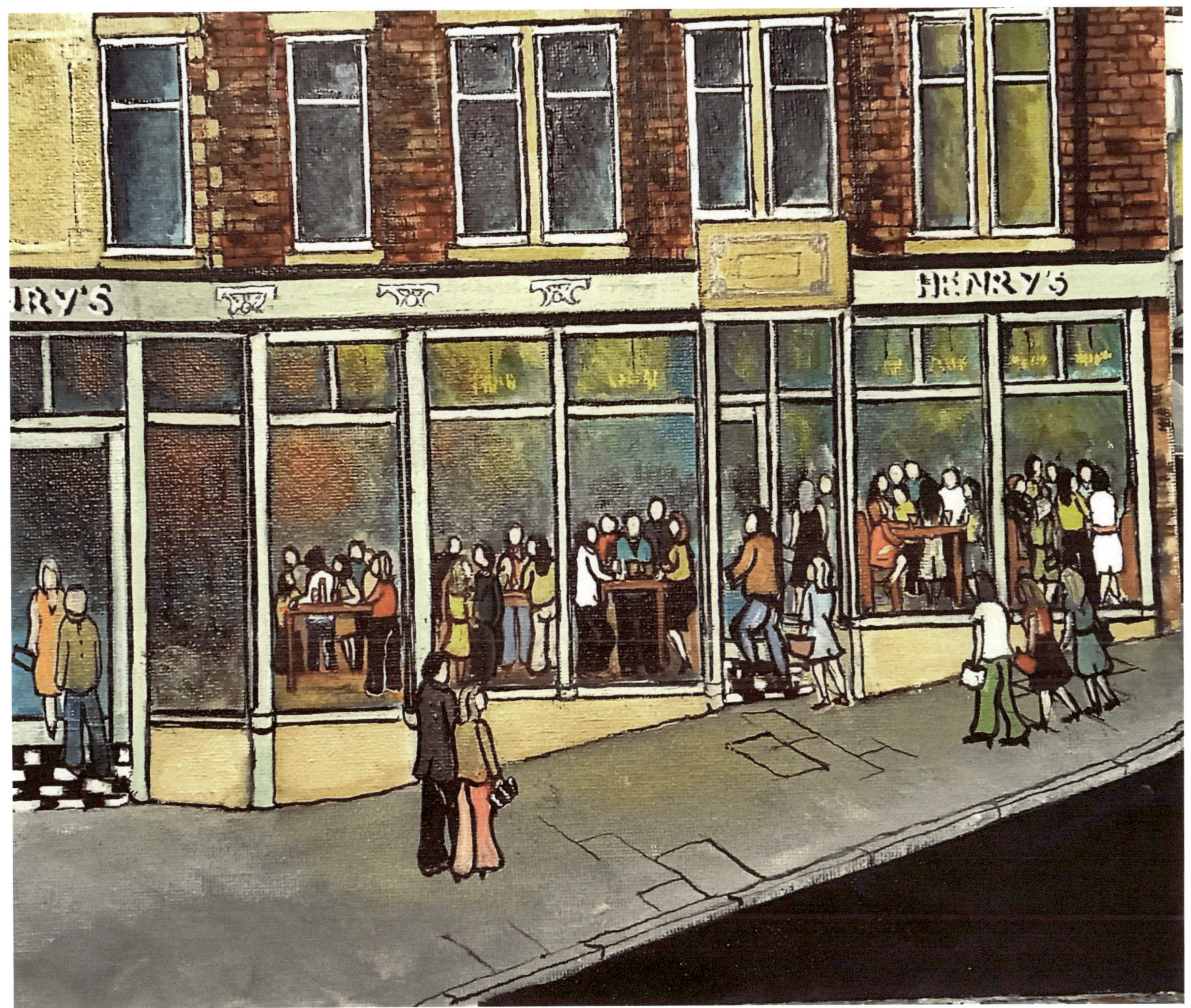
HENRY'S
HENRY'S

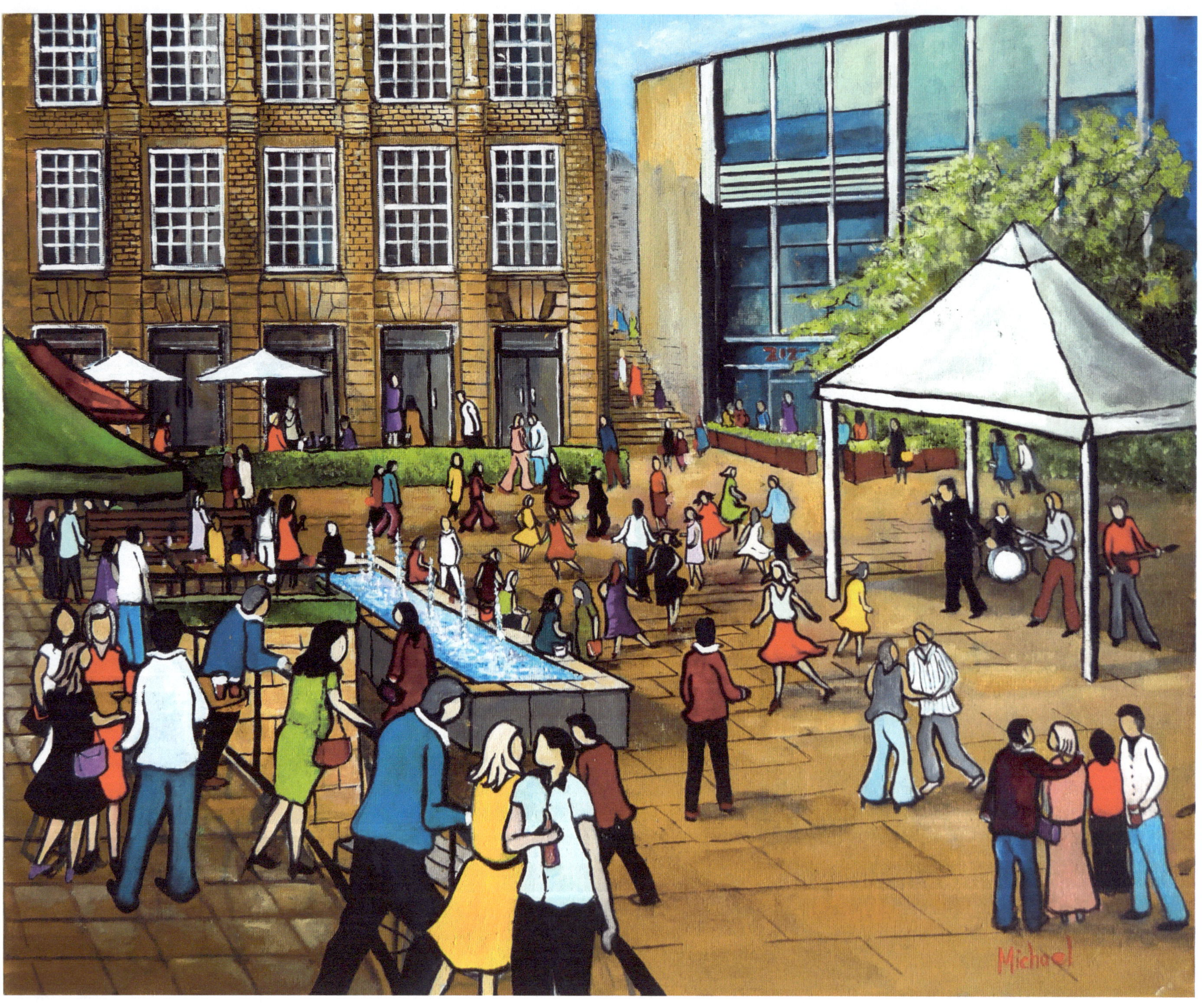
Michael

Leopold Square

(The present day)

Parkhill and Sheffield are now slowly but surely waking up, to new and hopefully exciting times. Vibrant and colourful, the people still enjoy themselves at every opportunity.

Canal Basin/ Victoria Quays Market

(The present day)

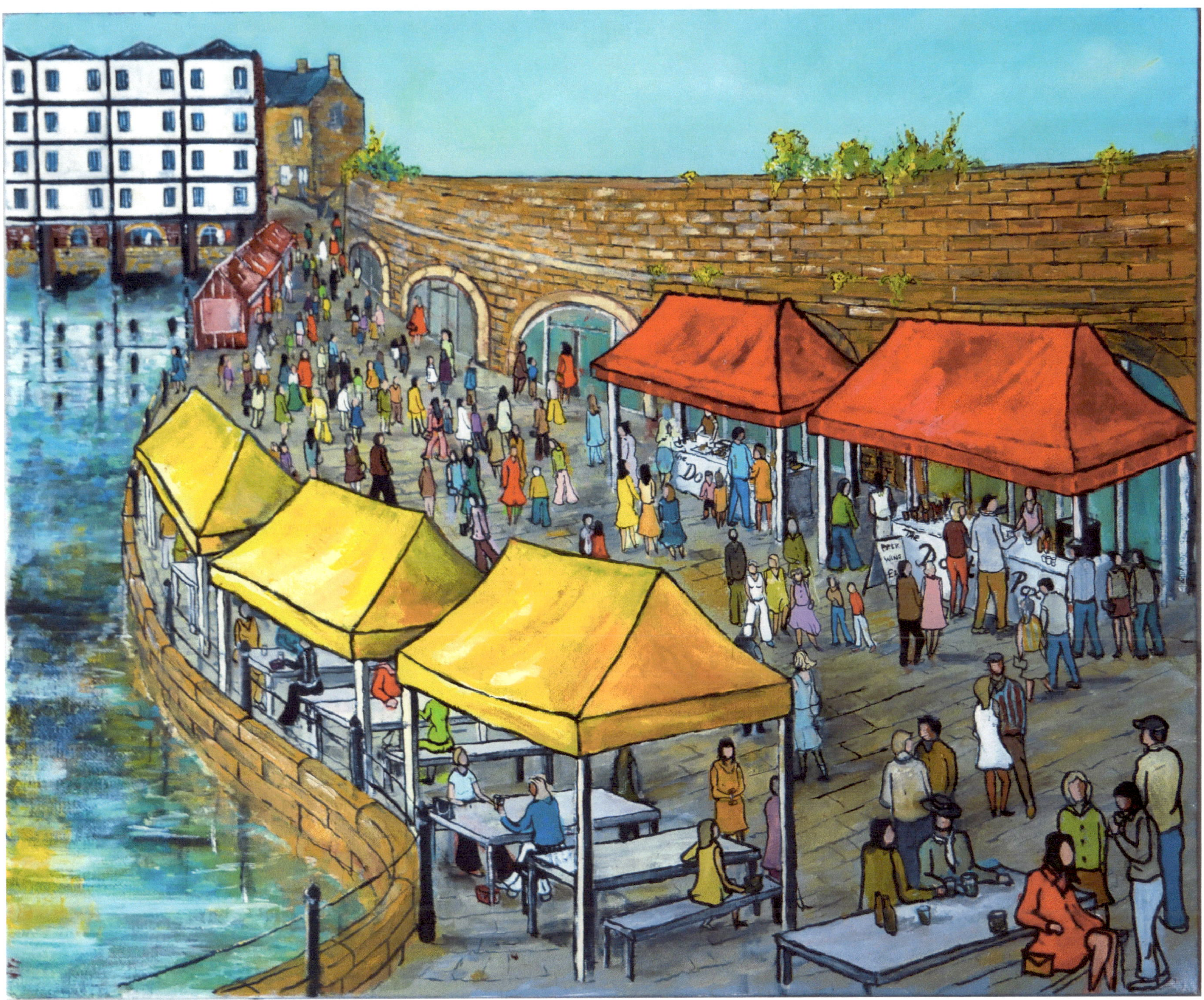

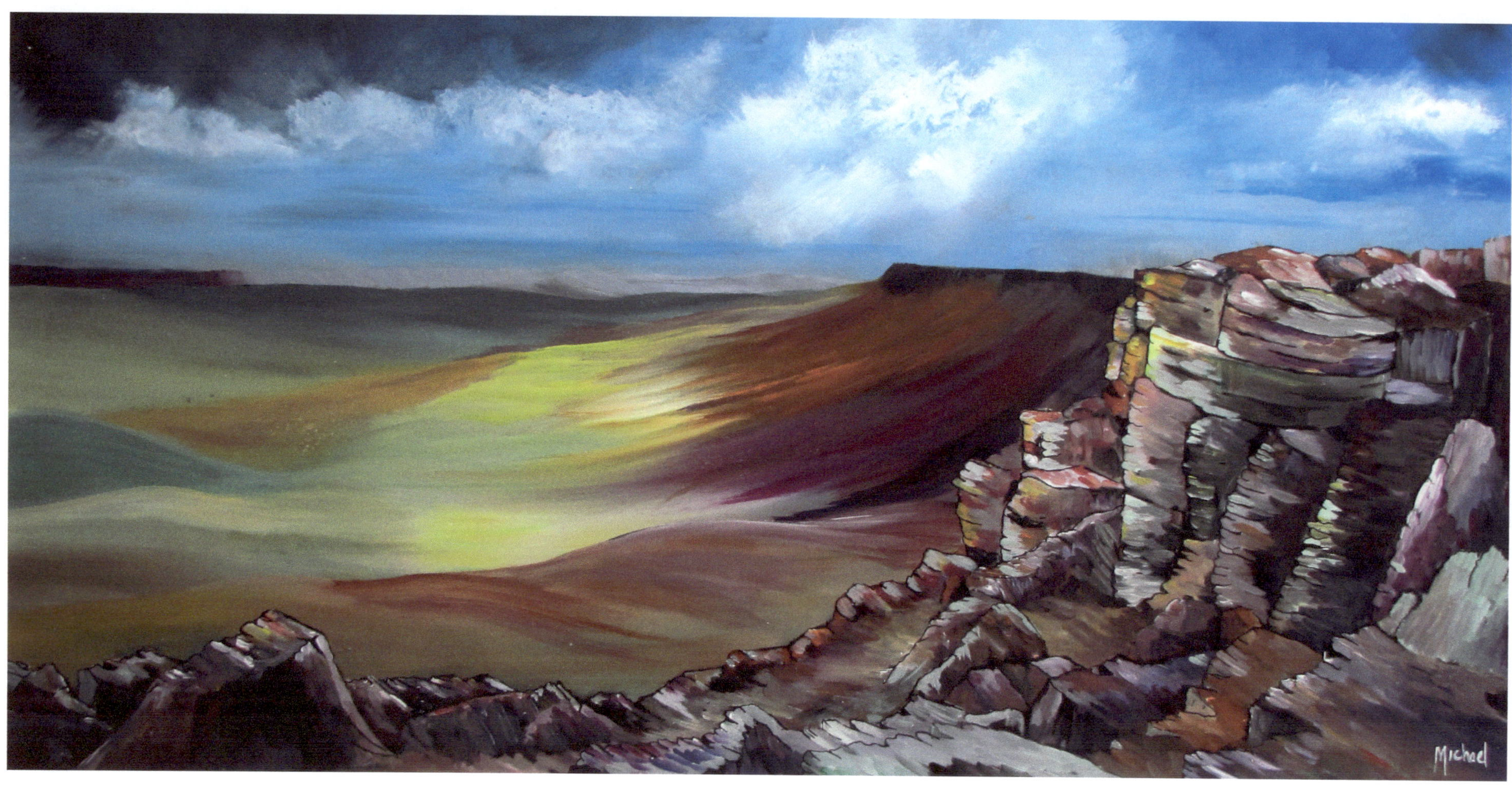

Sheffield is dubbed the Outdoor City. We're lucky to have the Peak District right on our doorstep, and some of it in the city boundary.
I swear when I was younger I don't recall ever going to places like Bakewell, or Chatsworth; the furthest I recall was the museum or Rivelin, occasionally.